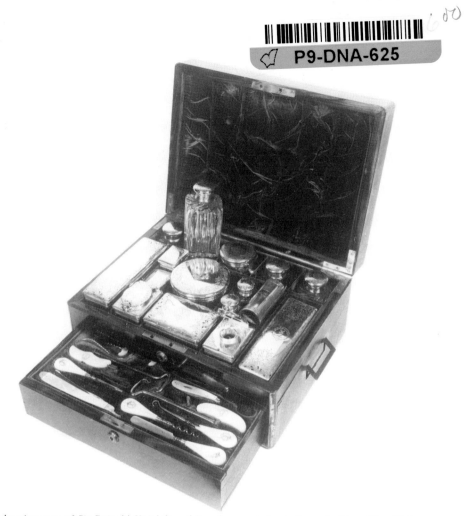

The dressing case of Sir Rainald Knightley of Fawsley, made by J. Bramah, Piccadilly. All items bear the Knightley crest, those of silver being hall-marked for 1841. The matching pieces with mother-of-pearl handles, such as buttonhook, boot-hooks, razor etc, are of the same date.

BUTTONHOOKS AND SHOEHORNS

Sue Brandon

Shire Publications Ltd

CONTENTS

Published in 1995 by Shire Publications Ltd, Cromwell House, Church Street, Princes Risborough, Buckinghamshire HP27 9AA, UK. Copyright © 1984 by Sue Brandon. First published 1984; reprinted 1987, 1991 and 1995. Shire Album 122. ISBN 0 85263 696 2.

Printed in Great Britain by CIT Printing Services, Press Buildings, Merlins Bridge, Haverfordwest, Dyfed SA61 1XF.

British Library Cataloguing in Publication Data: Brandon, Sue. Buttonhooks and shoehorns. — (Shire album; 122) 1. Buttonhooks — Collectors and collecting. 2. Shoehorns — Collectors and collecting. I. Title. 391'.45 NK4890.B8. ISBN 0-85263-696-2.

A variety of mother-of-pearl handled buttonhooks and looped buttoners. Some of these were probably originally matched with sewing tools such as a crochet hook and stiletto. The shield-shaped item with folding blade and buttonhook was made to hang on a gentleman's watch chain.

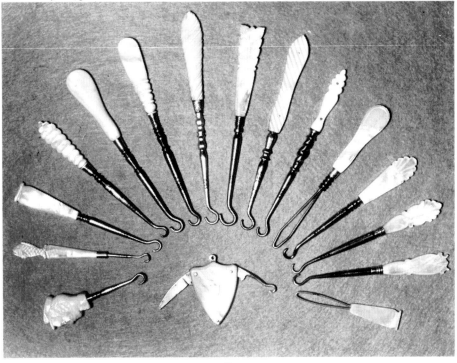

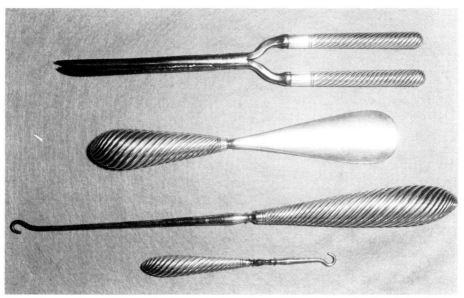

Set of German silver (.800), curling tongs, shoehorn (length 225 mm), buttonhook and glovehook, c 1900.

INTRODUCTION

Dressing and undressing is a process to which few of us today give much consideration. Modern styling and fabrics have removed this burden from us. Formal dress is rarely required, and a minimum of underwear is worn. Gloves (to complement an outfit, as opposed to giving warmth), have virtually disappeared from the fashion scene.

In the past dressing and undressing was a tedious and often uncomfortable procedure. Although fashion changed considerably during the century from 1830, it was always dominated, especially during the nineteenth century, by the quantity and complexity of the garments involved. The more affluent had a valet or ladies' maid to lay out the garments for the day with the appropriate underwear and accessories, and also to cope with the numerous tiresome fastenings. The

majority, however, struggled to be fashionable and maintain an air of gentility with the help of various aids, produced to assist with the wearing of all the items fashion demanded.

The correct gloves and footwear provided the finishing touch to a carefully selected outfit. A shoehorn eased the feet into snugly fitting boots or shoes, and a buttonhook was then required to fasten any buttons. Gloves were painstakingly drawn over each finger, and their tiny buttons secured with the help of a glovehook. Both buttonhooks and shoehorns had been in existence for centuries. It was, however, the Victorians (seldom using their fingers when an implement could be found to perform the task) who re-discovered and produced them in such great quantity and variety.

A family group photographed about 1913. The two girls wear button-boots, and the boy's boots are laced. The boy recalls, 'The button-boots were made of a lovely kid, and to do them up with the buttonhook was quite a task'.

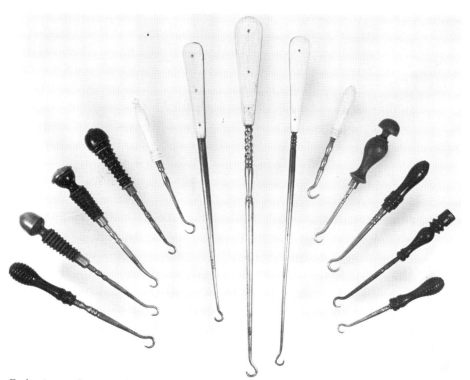

Early nineteenth century buttonhooks, with handles of wood and bone. The much-turned wooden handles possibly date from the Napoleonic wars. The three central examples have a piece of bone riveted on either side of the steel handle, which is a continuation of the buttonhook itself. The shafts of the steel hooks show a wide variety of shaping and turning.

BUTTONHOOKS

A buttonhook as we recognise it today is 'an instrument in the form of a hook, which is clasped round the buttons to pull them through the buttonholes'. This definition of a *tire-bouton* or *button-pull* was given in 1680. Yet the development of the buttonhook from a seventeenth-century buttoner to the many and varied styles of the nineteenth century is open to speculation. Its history remains fragmentary, though it naturally shadowed the use of buttons as fastenings for costume and costume accessories.

Buttons were mentioned in the fourteenth century as fastenings for footwear and, later, tunics. It was not until around 1550, when stout jerkins and doublets came into general use, that buttonhooks may have been required to fasten the tough leather. The first printed reference was in 1611: 'Boutonneur: A Buttoner; or an instrument — wherewith buttons are pulled through their o'er-strait holes' (*A Dictionarie of the French and English Tongues,* Randle Cotgrave). During the following 150 years, references to buttonhooks are scant. It is assumed that they survived through association with the military buff-coat, and the gaiters and leggings worn throughout that period by both the military and civilian population. Those which existed were probably quickly made up for use as the need arose, and as quickly discarded. It is difficult to date buttonhooks with confidence prior to the nineteenth century. Even after this, dating is not easy with non-silver handles, although turned bone

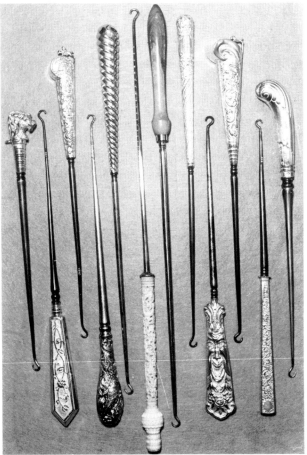

Large, late nineteenth century boot buttonhooks (lengths 305 mm - 480 mm), dated between 1882 and 1891. These would have been used mainly to fasten men's hunting and riding boots, but also by ladies, when quantities of underwear and tight clothing restricted bending. From left: London 1889, silver dog's head inscribed 'Tom'. London 1888. London 1882, silver horse and rider on top of handle. London 1891, heavy gilded handle with embossed birds, etc. Birmingham 1890. Long, elaborately carved Chinese ivory handle with silver-plated hook. Smooth boxwood handle. Birmingham 1888. London 1888. London 1888, silver horse on end of handle. Birmingham 1888. Sheffield 1889, pistol-grip handle.

or wooden handles are often of early nineteenth century origin. The popularity of men's button-boots in the 1830s initiated a more general demand for a fastening aid. From this date a steady increase can be noticed in the number of buttonhooks produced to cater for what was then almost exclusively a masculine market.

It seems most likely to have been the changes in feminine fashion which occasioned the late nineteenth century mass-production of the buttonhook. From about 1870, long and tightly fitting kid gloves were worn, and a small glovehook was most useful for fastening the tiny buttons. By 1880, ladies' button-boots, which had previously been soft and had

not presented any fastening problems, were made of stronger leather. Fashion decreed they should be pulled tight to show the shape of the ankle, so a buttonhook became an essential aid. Lines of small buttons on dress bodices were also more easily fastened with the help of a buttonhook. During this period people travelled more widely as communications improved. Buttonhooks were useful souvenirs of places visited, from exhibitions and world fairs, to the newly popular seaside resorts. Royal occasions, such as Queen Victoria's Jubilee in 1897, or the Coronation of Edward VII in 1902, all merited a buttonhook souvenir as a reminder of the event, both in Britain and the Empire.

RIGHT: *Assorted gold buttonhooks for female use. Many of the smaller glovehooks shown, including the folding examples, are entirely of gold. Two gold glovehooks illustrated have handles of banded agate. The looped buttoner is of gold and moonstones.*

BELOW: *Souvenir and commemorative glovehooks (lengths 50 mm - 70 mm). Top row from left: Chester 1913, kookaburra. Birmingham 1913, enamelled coat-of-arms of Australia. Birmingham 1914, map of Australia. Gilded, all-silver glovehook enamelled with coat-of-arms of 'Halifax Nova Scotia'. Sterling silver, inscribed 'Chicago 93' (to commemorate the World Fair). Gilded sterling silver, enamelled with initials 'B C' (British Columbia), and the words 'Semper Liber' around the veiled head of Queen Victoria. This was almost certainly produced to celebrate the Jubilee in 1897. Gilded silver wire twisted to coloured enamelled maple-leaf marked 'Canada'. Birmingham 1904, all-silver glovehook with town crest of 'Scarborough'. Birmingham 1909, all-silver souvenir from the Isle of Man. Bottom row: All-silver glovehook, showing map of Tasmania. Birmingham 1913, all-silver kookaburra. All-silver (sterling), Australian 3d piece dated 1910. Birmingham 1910, all-silver Welsh lady. Sheffield 1897, silver and mother-of-pearl fold-out glovehook with Manx symbol.*

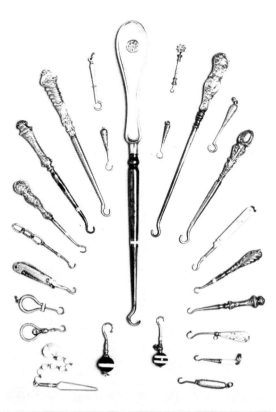

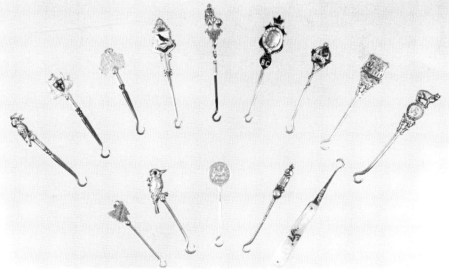

7

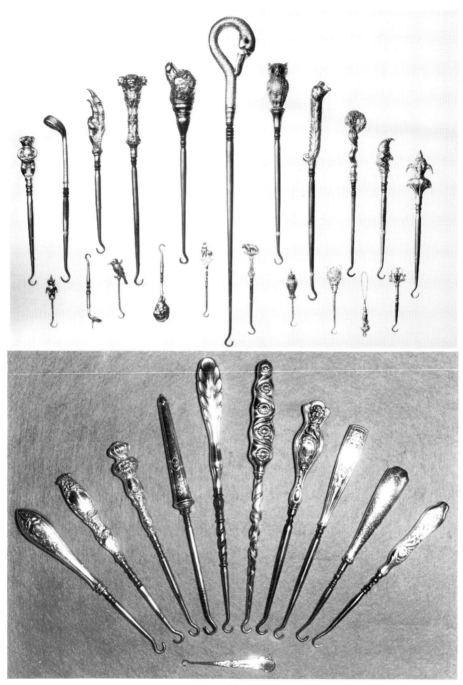

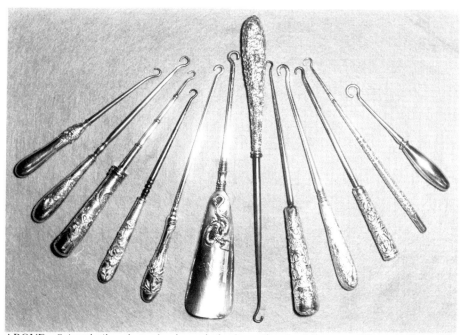

ABOVE: *Oriental silver buttonhooks and shoehorn (lengths 140 mm - 300 mm). From left: Japanese silver handle with superimposed design of foliage. Silver handle, bamboo design. All-silver (.800) dragon and bamboo design, marked 'Zeewo' plus Oriental characters. Japanese superimposed design of chrysanthemum flowers and leaves. All-silver, with superimposed bamboo palm, marked '90 WH' plus Oriental characters. All-silver combined buttonhook and shoehorn with superimposed dragon, marked 'LH 90' plus Oriental characters. Large, highly decorated Japanese handle, hollow, bearing Japanese symbols. Indian silver handle, with design of elephants, etc. All-silver design of Indian goddesses, etc. Indian silver handle. All-silver hollow, lightweight buttonhook with Oriental flower and leaf design. Plain, all-silver buttonhook, marked '90 SF' plus Oriental characters.*

OPPOSITE, TOP: *Silver-handled buttonhooks (lengths 155 mm - 355 mm). Some of the birds and animals have eyes of red glass. From left: Teddy bear, Birmingham 1913. Golf club, Birmingham 1910. Silver claw, Birmingham 1910. Pug dog, Birmingham 1908. Spaniel dog, Birmingham 1902. Swan's head, London 1888. Owl, Birmingham 1906. Leopard, date illegible. Heron, Birmingham 1895. Mr Punch, Birmingham 1904. Jester, Chester 1907. Bottom: Various unusual silver glovehooks.*

OPPOSITE, BOTTOM: *American silver handles, marked 'Sterling' plus sundry makers' marks; all with steel hooks. The buttonhooks vary in length from 160 mm to 225 mm and the all-silver glovehook is 75mm.*

Jewellers and silversmiths seem suddenly to have recognised the potential market which had opened up to them. With typical Victorian zeal and ingenuity the buttonhook, which had struggled on unnoticed for 200 years or more, was re-born in a wide variety of sizes, styles and materials, and found its way into almost every home in the land. Workshops, already producing handles for needlework tools, manicure items and cutlery, had no difficulty providing buttonhook handles. The mass-production techniques of the Industrial Revolution enabled them to meet the demand. Although French, Dutch and German buttonhooks can be found, it was chiefly in Britain and the USA that the greatest production took place. There are a large number of silver-handled buttonhooks available to the collector today. These were assayed chiefly in Birmingham, but

9

also in London, Chester and Sheffield. Some buttonhooks have an Oriental appearance, and were almost certainly made in India and other areas of the Far East for British colonial families.

The majority of buttonhooks have a fairly standard construction. A strong piece of steel, with a blunt hook at the end, is tightly fitted into a handle. This is secured with a resinous material which hardens so the hook is firmly embedded and can withstand the hard pulling required to fasten boot-buttons. The steel was not, of course, stainless, so the hooks themselves often rust and become discoloured. Many were originally plated with silver or chrome, or gilded, but this too tends to wear.

Buttonhooks vary in length from around 19 inches (483 mm) to those, barely 1 inch (25 mm) long, which were used to fasten glove buttons. These tiny glovehooks are often the exception to the use of a steel hook. Because they had a much lighter duty to perform, the hooks themselves might be of gold or silver, making them ornamental as well as useful. Apart from the variety of material used, buttonhooks could be anything from a simple piece of looped wire, to elaborate and costly designs in precious metal with handles shaped as birds or animals. There were folding and combination buttonhooks, and ingenious and novelty examples. Military, commemorative, souvenir and advertising items abound, each variation produced to fulfil a particular need.

Five brass shoelifts, dating between 1830 and 1850.

Below: Cattle horn shoehorn (length 635 mm), dated 1599 and inscribed 'MAYE'. Bottom: Cattle horn shoehorn (length 190 mm), dated 1611, and hooked and pierced for suspension. This shoehorn is reputed to have been through the Battle of Waterloo.

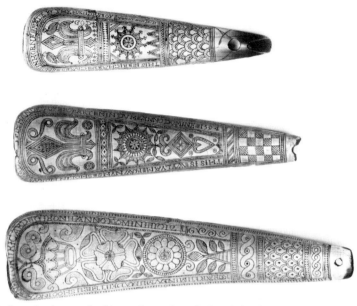

Robart Mindum shoehorns of white ox-horn. Inscribed and dated. Top: 'This is Richard Crabs shoein horne made by the handes of Robart Mindum. God 1595'. The end is hooked and pierced for suspension, overall length 160 mm. Centre: 'This is Wylyam Rownyns shoein horne made by the handes of Robart Mindum. Anno Domine 1594'. Length 180 mm. Bottom: 'Robart Mindum made this shooing horne for Richard Gibon. Anno Domini 1612'. Length 220 mm.

SHOEHORNS OR SHOELIFTS

A shoehorn is an aid for helping the shoe on to the foot. Evidence points to a piece of cow-hide with the hair on one side being used throughout history for this purpose. Shoehorns continued in this form, alongside later variations, for many centuries. They certainly existed in the middle ages, although details about their use and distribution are scarce. By the sixteenth century other materials, such as horn, were in use. The natural curve of the horn was ideally shaped to cradle the heel and ease it into the shoe, and the name *shoehorn* persists today even though the term *shoelift* is technically more correct.

Elizabethan shoes were tight-fitting and would have required a shoehorn, and evidence of the time shows that these were kept at roadside inns for use by the patrons. In 1579, the City of Exeter records show 'A showg horn of iron . . .

6d', adding yet another material to those previously mentioned. Robart Mindum was a maker of highly decorated shoehorns in the late sixteenth and early seventeenth centuries. Examples of his work are easily recognised by the elaborate floral and geometric designs and the date and lettering which are engraved on all his shoehorns. These were originally stained to contrast with the white ox-horn. Shakespeare, in *Troilus and Cressida* (Act V Scene 1), refers to 'a thrifty shoeing-horn on a chain hanging at his brother's leg'. However, by the late seventeenth century, as shoe fashions changed and the need declined, shoehorns became fewer in number and less elaborate. In the eighteenth century shoehorns were made in many patterns, from iron and brass as well as natural materials. *Savary's Commercial Dictionary* of 1741 describes the continuing use

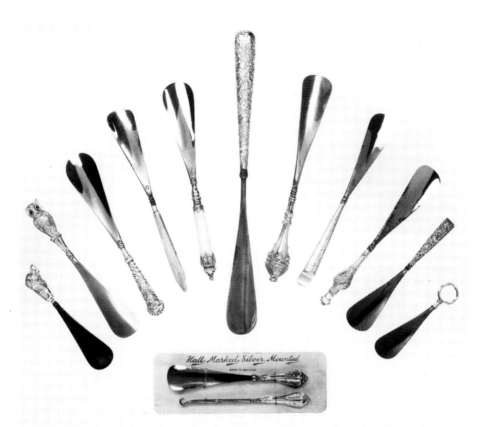

ABOVE: *Silver handled shoehorns (lengths 130 mm - 370 mm). From left: Birmingham 1903, dog's head. Birmingham 1906, owl with red glass eyes. Birmingham 1890. London 1932, blue enamel on silver. Birmingham 1894, ivory with silver mounts. Birmingham 1890. Birmingham 1907, yellow glass thistle inset. Birmingham 1901. Birmingham 1915, looped silver handle. Bottom, set of buttonhook and shoehorn on original card, Chester 1920.*

OPPOSITE, TOP: *Late nineteenth century and early twentieth century shaped shoehorns. From left: Bent leg of light alloy material (length 145 mm). Straight leg of solid copper (230 mm). Polished steel leg (240 mm). Small shoe-shaped light alloy shoehorn (105 mm). Leg shape in wood with painted shoe (190 mm). Victorian brass leg showing 'bloomer' leg and button-boot (240 mm).*

OPPOSITE, BOTTOM: *Various pocket combinations. The top three show a steel buttonhook which either swivels across the plastic shoehorn or is joined to it with a ring. Those on the right also include a suede hat-brush, while the centre one is similar, with the addition of a clothes brush. The various items fold compactly together and swivel out individually as required. The set of plastic-handled shoehorn, buttonhook and comb fit neatly into a plastic carrying case.*

RIGHT: *Novelty French shoehorn of early plastic, marked DEPOSEE. The pierrot's head swivels to reveal the steel buttonhook.*

13

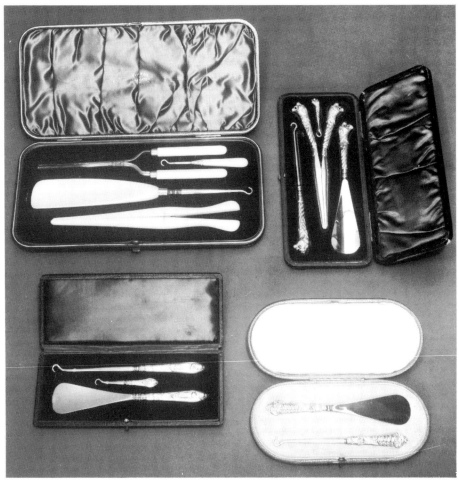

Four boxed presentation sets. Top left: Set from Finnigan's, Deansgate, Manchester, ivory-handled glove-stretchers, shoehorn and combined steel buttonhook (length 270 mm), glovehook with silver hook and collar dated London 1891, and curling tongs. This set was intended for a gentleman, the tongs being used to curl moustaches. Top right: Ladies' boxed set, Birmingham 1900, containing buttonhook (length 180 mm), glove-stretchers, shoehorn and all-silver glovehook. All the items have handles shaped as leopard's heads, set with red glass 'cabochon' eyes. Bottom left: Set of buttonhook, glovehook and shoehorn (170 mm), London 1903 (imported). Bottom right: 9ct gold buttonhook and shoehorn (length 155 mm) with gilded steel hook and horn, Birmingham 1898.

of cow-hide: 'a thin soft piece of fur, usually calf's skin, with the hair left on, which the shoemakers make use of when they get their customers to try on shoes'. As all footwear until the nineteenth century was handmade, it would have been quite usual for shoemakers to keep a shoehorn for this purpose.

Few early shoehorns exist today outside museums. None of cow-hide appear to have survived, due to natural deterioration and lack of contemporary interest in preserving such an easily replaced item. Other materials have fared better, and some interesting shoehorns can be seen in museums

14

Shoehorns and buttonhooks combined (lengths 205 mm - 315 mm). From left: London 1930 (imported .925), silver shoehorn (80 mm) with steel glovehook concealed in the tassel. Birmingham 1910. Birmingham 1910. London 1905, ivory handle with silver mount and initials. Birmingham 1900. Birmingham 1888, ivory shoehorn and steel buttonhook. Birmingham 1911. London 1913. Birmingham 1907. Birmingham 1899, one-piece all-silver combination. Sheffield 1913, all-silver foldover, 255 mm extended.

throughout Britain. They were in use in many parts of the world. For example the oldest Swedish shoehorn is in the Nordista Museum and dates from 1627. By the nineteenth century, with fashion dictating tightly fitting footwear for both men and women, shoehorns were again commonplace. It is these later examples which the collector is most likely to find today. Horn, ivory, silver, brass and steel were all employed, with large curled brass shoehorns being popular in Victorian times. Twentieth century examples are frequently of various plastics and often bear the name of the shoeshop or firm which gave them away for advertising purposes. Matched with buttonhooks and other items, shoehorns were commonplace in fitted travelling-cases. The *Harrods Catalogue* of 1895, in the section headed 'Bags, Trunks and Portmanteaus', illustrates examples for both gentlemen and ladies. Boxed sets appear under the heading 'Useful Presents'. A

set of 'Silver Handle Button Hook and Shoe Lift, and Glove Button Hook, in Morocco and velvet-lined case' cost 22s 6d. *Lady's Pictorial* of 1889 describes the marriage of Maude, the eldest daughter of the Chancellor of the Exchequer, 'which was witnessed by a large and fashionable audience'. Among the many gifts was a buttonhook. Another society bride had been given a case containing two silver buttonhooks, shoehorn, curling tongs and glove stretchers, plus several other gifts of single buttonhooks. Delighted though the recipients must have been, there is a limit to the number of such items required by even the most fashionable couple, and there seems little doubt that many sets were seldom, if ever, used. They therefore survive, sometimes in mint condition, to the present day.

In many ways, the use of shoehorns shadowed that of buttonhooks, and the two items were often combined in various ways. The earliest silver examples date from the 1880s and have an ornate central handle, with ivory shoehorn at one end and steel buttonhook at the other. Similar twentieth century examples tend to be shorter and plainer, and both shoehorn and buttonhook are usually made of steel. In some combinations the buttonhook swivels neatly across the shoehorn, enabling it to fit compactly in the pocket. The shoehorn might be of silver, brass, steel, aluminium, tortoiseshell, horn or various plastics. Any of these combination items could be enclosed in a case of cloth, leather or plastic, and might occasionally include a suede hat-brush or clothes-brush.

Some items which would have required a buttonhook to aid the fastening. Top row: Early twentieth century cloth gaiters with seventeen buttons and leather straps that buckled under the instep of the boots or shoes. A boxed pair of cloth spats of similar date from Hope brothers. Centre row: Child's china sock-driers or boot-warmers (when placed inside the boots and filled with hot water). Child's button-over shoe, late Victorian. Pair of child's white kid boots with pearl buttons, c 1885. Single black button-boot dating from 1890 - 1910. Child's buttonhook. Bottom row: Men's black leather button-boots, early 1920s, Wheatsheaf trade mark on sole. Leather button-boots with cloth tops (possibly American), 1915 - 1920s.

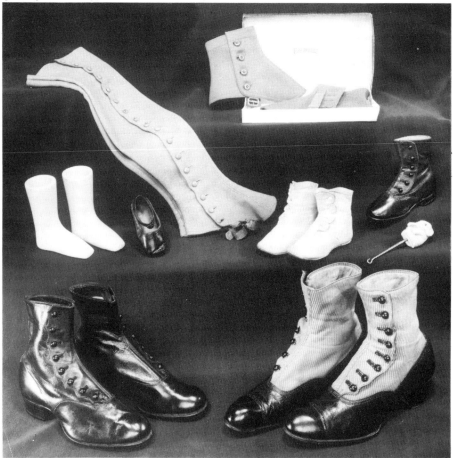

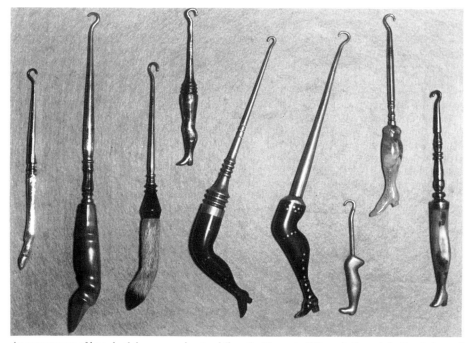

An assortment of legs, both human and animal (lengths 90 mm to 255 mm). From left: Deer's leg and hoof in silver, Birmingham 1888. Horn, carved into hoof shape. Black plastic imitation chamois horn with natural hair. One piece steel hook and leg shape, with inlaid copper sections. Two 'naughty nineties' legs of brass and bois durci (an early plastic), with brass rivets defining the buttons on the boots. Small pewter leg. Clear yellow plastic leg with button-boot (intended to imitate amber). One piece steel hook and leg with horn-faced sides and copper boot.

A HELPING HAND FOR ALL

Required by men, women and children, buttonhooks found their way into every level of society. The strong steel hook being common to almost all examples, only the design and material of the handle distinguished the wealthy owner from the poor. It is this spectrum of usage which gives buttonhooks a special place among items of personal use, and provides us with a small but significant insight into the social history of the time. Shoehorns, though not as widely used as buttonhooks in the nineteenth century, were commonplace in many homes. Button-boots, a practical fashion outdoors, were often replaced by close-fitting shoes or patent leather pumps for inside or evening wear. A shoehorn, kept in pock-et or purse, enabled the change to be quickly and neatly achieved.

GENTLEMEN

Early Victorian buttonhooks were made with masculine appeal. Wealthy gentlemen would possess stylish dressing cases for travelling, fitted with every conceivable toilet item including buttonhook and shoehorn, these often combined as one piece and made of steel. A glove buttonhook, with bone or ivory handle, might also be included among matching manicure items, razors, and perhaps even curling tongs for the magnificent moustaches sported by gentlemen of the day.

Riding boots were often a problem

Some nineteenth century steel buttonhooks with handles carved from the South American corozo nut, or vegetable ivory. The two parrots have a certain charm, but the human faces tend to be rather grotesque. All have appropriate glass eyes, and would probably have been made largely for male use (lengths 85 mm to 190 mm).

both to put on and to remove, so a portable set, containing all the necessary aids, was available. It took the form of a wooden boot-jack which, when opened and placed on the ground, provided a recess into which the heel of the boot could be placed and the boot levered off. Hollows inside concealed buttonhook, leather punch and a pair of boot-hooks. A successful hunt would result in a kill, and many trophies, such as stag hooves or antlers, were used as buttonhook handles.

As early as 1816, Sheffield manufacturers were producing 'pocket cutlery' with a buttonhook attachment among the other necessities such as numerous blades, corkscrews and manicure items. Later they became standard inclusions in various specialist knives until the 1940s. Other pocket combinations were also popular. One took the form of a strong horseshoe shape in steel. The tools folded away and included every gadget that a gentleman might require, such as a hoof-pick, buttonhook, gimlet, corkscrew, carriage-key and screwdriver.

Although buttonhooks were never issued as official items of army equipment, they might have been used by a batman dressing an officer. Many buttonhooks and shoehorns were made by men in the services as keepsakes for wives and sweethearts. The First World War produced large numbers of these handmade commemorative artefacts. The most common examples have handles made of multi-coloured bands of varying materials, which were threaded on to the tang of the buttonhook and then turned and shaped. Occasionally these incorporate a cartridge case, or are topped with a regimental badge or button. These would have been made, presumably unofficially, at corps workshops, or during quieter periods in the fighting in the front line.

Buttoned gaiters were popular from the late Victorian period until the 1930s, and this extended the useful life of the buttonhook long after button-boots themselves ceased to be fashionable. It was usual for the clergy to wear gaiters, the buttons of which would undoubtedly have required a buttonhook. Shorter gaiters, or spats, were worn to protect shoes from dirt and mud. Made in various colours, they were fastened under the

18

instep of the shoe with a leather strap, and buttoned on one side of the foot and ankle.

Gentlemen also required an aid to fasten glove buttons, stiff shirt fronts and waistcoat buttons, and to cope with the awkward fastenings on starched and celluloid collars popular in the early twentieth century. A small looped buttoner — similar to a buttonhook, but with a closed loop instead of a hook — was frequently used for these tasks. The looped end was pushed through the buttonhole and caught round the shank of the button which was then easily pulled through. These could be attached to a watch-chain or key-ring, and were also useful for glove buttons. In town, a gentleman would wear or carry gloves of kid or doeskin, and before leading a lady on to the dance floor he would always button on a pair of white gloves. A buttonhook, or buttoner, would be an essential aid on these occasions, as would a shoehorn to effect a speedy change from button-boots to patent pumps for dancing.

LADIES

It was not until the 1880s that ladies required buttonhooks to fasten their boots. At this time, a small hand and foot were taken to be a sign of gentility, and many a Victorian lady was prepared to endure footwear that was too small in the hope of making her feet appear more ladylike. By the end of the century high boots, fastened with about sixteen but-

Various folding steel and combination buttonhooks. Top row: An assortment of fold-over buttonhooks to be kept in handbag or pocket; one combined with a small corkscrew, and another (centre top) combined with corkscrew and carriage key. Centre: Three multiple penknives. Bottom row: Plastic covered cylindrical etui with four slide-up tools comprising buttonhook, knife blade, nail cleaner and propelling pencil. All the remaining examples have brass cases (some painted black and inset with small turquoise stones), and contain two, three or four similar items. Hung on a watch chain etc, these 'etuis' were used by both gentlemen and ladies, throughout the Victorian and Edwardian period.

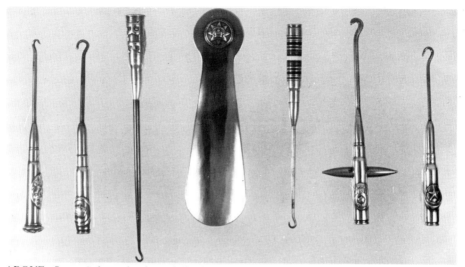

ABOVE: *Souvenir buttonhooks and shoehorn made around the time of the First World War by soldiers, using rifle cartridges, bullets and other materials to hand. In America such artefacts are known as 'Trench Art'. From left: The first two cartridge cases are decorated with service buttons, and the third with Royal Engineers insignia and General Service style button. It is inscribed 'Le Monument, Baupaume, Juillet 1917'. The shoehorn is made from a piece of scrap brass, possibly a shellcase. Of the remaining three, the first is a banded cartridge case, the second is decorated with a Canadian Expeditionary Force button, and the third with a Turkish button (lengths 140 mm - 180 mm).*

BELOW: *Early twentieth-century advertisement for the 'Zenith' collar buttoners made by Lambourne and Company, manufacturing jewellers, Birmingham. Examples of the 'Zenith' and 'Empire' buttoners are shown at the bottom of the photograph including one with a bone handle advertising 'C J Hardy & Co Ltd, Hosiers, Leeds'. This includes a grooved end which forms a 'collar edge smoother'. Other buttoners are shown on the right. From top: 'The Rapid' collar buttoner (made in Germany) and advertising 'J Race 17 Oxford St Manchester'; the 'Croft' collar buttoner; collar buttoner, G T & Co London; 'Utryet' Lion Make.*

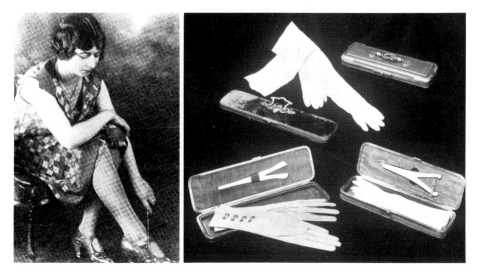

LEFT: *1926 photograph of a lady using a buttonhook to fasten her leopard skin shoes.*
RIGHT: *Four glove boxes c 1880 - 1910. In order to avoid the social disgrace of appearing in soiled gloves, a lady would take several pairs with her when travelling. The 'love-knot' handle (top right) is typical of many leather covered expanding glove boxes. Frequently, glove stretchers of bone or ivory are fitted inside the lid, and sometimes kept in place (bottom right) by a gilt fastening. When unscrewed and removed, the looped end serves as a glove buttoner. The two glove boxes on the left are not expanding, and the top example is velvet covered with an elaborate brass handle. The long white kid gloves have the short wrist fastening common at the end of the nineteenth century, whilst the tan leather gloves fasten with press-studs.*

tons, were worn for walking or travelling, as well as the energetic activities such as cycling and tennis in which women had begun to take part.

Cloth gaiters, buttoning up the side of the leg, were worn over boots, especially in winter. In her book *The Hills Of Home*, Amy Stewart Fraser recalls: 'Indoors, my mother wore black slippers with buckles, and in cold weather added calf-length gaiters which had to be patiently fastened button by button with a special hook'. By the twentieth century, shorter spats were being worn over dark-coloured shoes, although boots were still preferred for outdoor wear by most ladies. Later, when bar-shoes became popular, a shoehorn was used to ease them on, and a buttonhook still invariably employed to fasten even a single button.

During the nineteenth century, buttons appeared in profusion on ladies' clothing and also on gloves, which, through the ages, have been an essential accessory to feminine fashion. With the Victorian cult of gentility, gloves were an important means of expression. One romantic belief of the time, held by Lord Byron among others, was that a small and delicate hand was a sure sign of noble birth. Most long gloves from about 1835 onwards show a short opening only, buttoning over the wrist with four buttons. These could be unfastened and the gloves slipped back over the hands, but not entirely removed, for afternoon tea. A letter to *The Queen*, in 1862 pronounced: 'In every costume but the most extreme neglige a lady cannot be said to be dressed except she is nicely and completely gloved; and this applies equally to morning, afternoon, dinner and evening dress'. Not to wear gloves in church was considered particularly reprehensible. Even at the height of summer a lady never went out without her gloves, as only 'common' people who worked in the open air had sunburnt faces and rough un-gloved hands.

With the aid of glove-stretchers and

BELOW: *Small glovehooks (shown with a 50p piece). From left: Brass hook set with cut glass citrine. All-silver, Birmingham 1921, inset with mottled agate. All-silver with amethyst glass thistle inset. Silver hook and mount, Birmingham 1895, with mother-of-pearl handle. Silver hook, Birmingham 1897, with shaped goldstone handle. Silver hook, Birmingham 1887, with moonstone handle. All-silver hook and thistle shaped handle with small glass amethyst inset. Silver hook and mount, Birmingham 1914, with pointed amethyst handle. Nineteenth century cut-steel glovehook. Brass hook, with handle formed by two green scarab beetle cases. All-silver, Birmingham 1905, hook and handle inset with green shamrock design. Brass hook with carved coral handle. Nineteenth century, all-silver looped buttoner, handle inset with mother-of-pearl. All-silver, Birmingham 1892, looped buttoner. Cut-steel buttoner with gilded design on handle. All-silver, Birmingham 1898. All-silver, Birmingham 1897, twig shaped glovehook. Brass hook, inset with flat yellow cut-glass stone. Brass hook with clear cut-glass ball. Brass hook with grey striped agate ball. Brass hook inset with amethyst glass thistle. Centre: Miniature brass buttonhook and linked silver buttonhook, scissors and penknife. Too small for practical use, these may have been made as charms or small cracker gifts, or perhaps to accompany a Victorian china doll, often equipped in miniature with every accessory a fashionable young lady of the day would have required.*

ABOVE: *Mid-Victorian cut-steel chatelaine, a fashion by then more decorative than useful, but which had its origins in the bunch of keys which a medieval housewife wore at her girdle. This example carries many useful items such as a letter opener, writing tablet, pencil, pincushion, notebook, scissors, sovereign purse, penknife and folding buttonhook. A variety of other glovehooks, with hanging loops enabling them to be hung from a watch-chain or chatelaine, are also shown.*

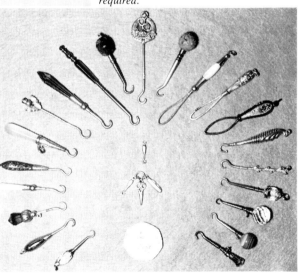

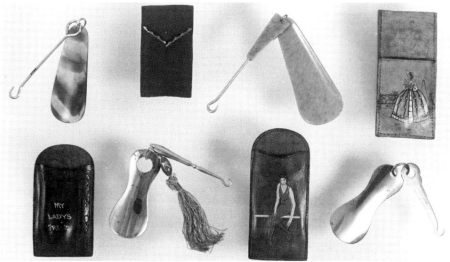

ABOVE: *Ladies' purse or pocket companions, 1920s to 1930s. Top, from left: Mottled plastic shoehorn linked to a steel wire buttonhook, with grosgrain carrying case. Green plastic shoehorn linked to matching buttonhook, with leather case. Bottom: Two types of linked steel buttonhooks and shoehorns with leather cases, one inscribed 'My Lady's Friend', and the other illustrating a shoehorn in use.*

BELOW: *Silver handled buttonhooks (lengths 175 mm - 240 mm), dated from 1919 to 1928. From left: Birmingham 1919. Chester 1920. Birmingham 1921. Birmingham 1922. Birmingham 1923, gilded silver with blue enamel. London 1924, gilded handle. London 1925, blue enamel. Birmingham 1926. Birmingham 1926, blue enamel. Sheffield 1928, Art Deco style. Birmingham 1928, coffee-coloured enamel.*

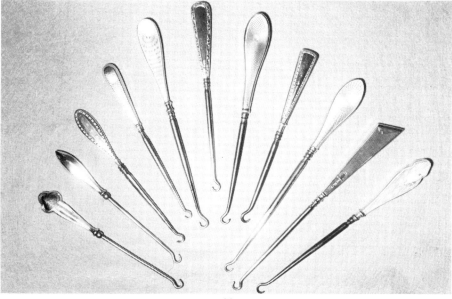

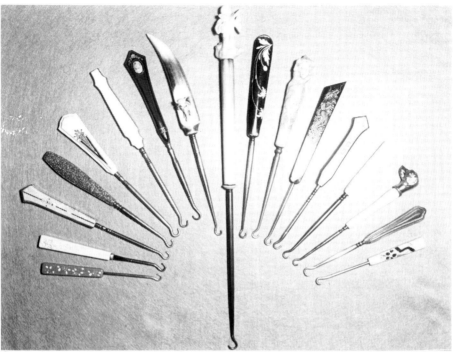

Group of 1920s and 1930s plastic handles, many showing the popular Art Deco shapes and designs of the period. Some of the plastics attempt to imitate natural materials such as shagreen (a type of un-tanned leather), fourth from left; ivory, eighth from left; or tortoiseshell, sixth from right; but such imitations are unlikely to deceive.

French chalk, ladies forced their hands into small size gloves to ensure a tight fit. The buttons were then fastened by a glovehook, the use of which also prevented the fingers from soiling the delicate fabric. Many silver or gold glovehooks qualified as items of jewellery, and were hung on watch-chains and chatelaines. Miniature glovehooks appeared on charm bracelets, and could sometimes be found in Christmas crackers. An upright cylindrical case, or *etui,* carried various useful items, and glovehooks were frequently included in late Victorian and Edwardian examples, with each item being slid out as required.

Buttonhooks, especially those with ivory, bone or mother-of-pearl handles, are often found in sewing sets of the day. They would be included so that when buttonholes were being made, they could be quickly and easily tested for size with the actual button to be used. Silver glovehooks and long boot-buttonhooks of the 1880s are some of the earliest which can be dated from the hallmark. A popular pattern could, however, be continued for many years, making it difficult for a collector to link some designs to a particular date. As a very general rule, silver-handled buttonhooks and shoehorns tended to be heavily ornamented, with much *repoussé* work, in the 1880s and 1890s. This was followed by the flowing lines of the *Art Nouveau* movement, typified in Britain by Liberty, and by Tiffany in the USA. It included the Celtic revival of designers such as Charles Rennie Mackintosh in Glasgow. Many of the silver handles shaped as animals, people and objects were made during the first decade of the twentieth century. Those made after 1914 were much simpler in style, and less highly decorated. Many were included in dressing-table sets, and incorporated col-

24

oured enamel in the design. Late examples, also frequently enamelled, show the angular designs and influence of the 1930s *Art Deco* period. This progression of style is only a generalisation, as it inevitably depended upon the whims of individual manufacturers or silversmiths.

CHILDREN

Children were not spared the wearing of button-boots, and some were obliged to do so long after boots had ceased to be fashionable, because they were reputed to strengthen weak ankles. In her book *The Button Box and other Essays* Alison Uttley gives this heartfelt recollection: 'There was a race against time in the morning to sew a button on my shoes before I left for school, for a button would fly off as I struggled with the buttonhook, and wrestled with the little black buttons, so buttoned boots were unpopular.' Not only had Victorian and Edwardian children to contend with uncomfortable footwear, but they were also heavily over-dressed. Their clothes were replicas of those of their parents, with all the accompanying bodices, linings, drawers and petticoats, not forgetting a hat, and cotton or kid gloves.

Gaiters and leggings were worn by children well into the 1930s, and as with button-boots they do not seem to have been very popular. Therle Hughes recalls in her book *Edwardiana for Collectors:* 'My own especial childhood misery was a pair of inherited leather gaiters buttoned tightly all down my protesting legs with a hostile buttonhook, from a silver-handled set of hook, shoehorn, and glove stretcher'. A few buttonhooks do exist that were made specifically for a child to use. Some depict nursery rhyme characters, and yet another has a cheerful red plastic elephant fixed atop the steel hook. These and others, sometimes paired with a shoehorn, would probably have been given to encourage a child to tackle its own buttons, but silver handles, shaped as teddy-bears and other animals would undoubtedly have been considered too good for a child, and reserved for adult use.

It was common for a buttonhook or

Group of buttonhooks and a shoehorn, suitable for a child to use (lengths 65 mm - 160 mm), and all with steel hooks unless otherwise stated. From left: Brown stained ivory bear with glass eyes. Boy's face, composition. Brass, Cat and the Fiddle. Brass Pixie. Mary Mary Quite Contrary in brass. Brass elephant. Painted brass robin, cat and parrot. All-brass owl. Red plastic elephant. Centre: Painted plastic shoehorn of crinolined lady, matched with buttonhook of tall-hatted Victorian gentleman.

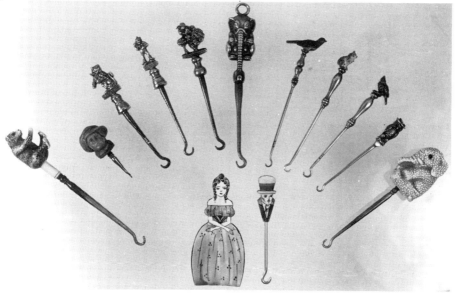

shoehorn to be available in the home for everyone in the family to use. It would have been kept somewhere handy, such as on the mantelpiece or as one lady recounted, 'hanging by the kitchen range with the curl rags'. The family buttonhook or shoehorn was plain, sturdy and practical rather than decorative, sometimes incorporating a loop for it to be hung from a convenient hook. Examples with heavy brass handles, often matching items such as the fire-irons, were frequently brought back from holidays and excursions, and proudly displayed by the fireplace.

Three early nineteenth century advertisements together with a selection of all-steel advertisement buttonhooks. Clockwise from top: 'The Wood-Milne Rubber Heel Pads'. 'Wear Smith's Boots and Shoes'. 'Dr Lovelace's Soap, Purest — Best'. 'Use Nugget Polishes'. 'David Easton, Practical Bootmaker'. 'Public Benefit Boot Co'. 'Frank Bentall, Kingston-on-Thames'. 'Walk Over Shoes'. 'T. Robinson, Altrincham'. 'Wear Benefit Shoes'.

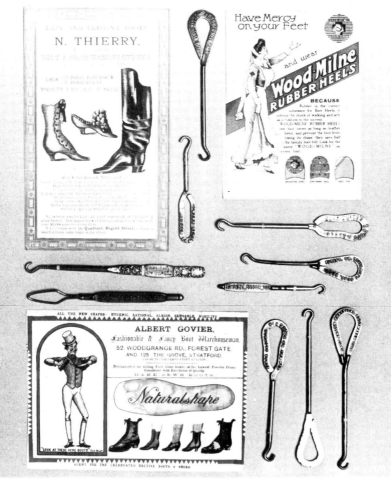

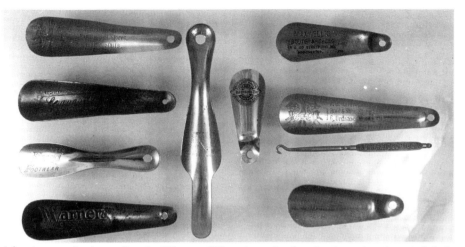

Advertisement shoehorns (lengths 100 mm - 220 mm), made of steel unless otherwise stated. Left: 'J. W. Darlington, Family Boot Stores, Audley, Staffs'. 'Lennards, For Good Boots and Shoes'. 'Wear "Pilot" Footwear'. 'Warners Footwear Ltd Branches Everywhere'. Centre: 'Lotus Shoes, Fitting in Every Sense'. Brass shoehorn, 'Harry Hall, Tailor and Habit Maker', with the reverse side bearing the words 'Good Luck'. Right: 'Maxwell's Boots and Shoes, 18 & 20 Stretford Rd, Manchester'. Shoehorn and buttonhook advertising 'R. B. Harridge & Co Boot and Shoe Stores. Estab 1849. Agent for Nugget Polishes'. 'J. W. Knowles Boot Repairer 112 Portwood St. Stockport'. ' "Kiwi" the Quality Boot Polish'.

ADVERTISING AND PATENTS

Advertising increased greatly during Queen Victoria's reign, and many firms used small items to carry their name and message. Buttonhooks and shoehorns, used daily in almost every home, were ideal for the purpose. Large numbers were produced and, though bearing the names of British firms, the majority were made in the USA. Most were of two standard shapes. Formed from one piece of steel, they had either a looped or straight handle, flattened to allow space for the name and message. Such advertising items were usually given away in shoeshops, drapers and haberdashers.

As would be expected, advertisements concerning footwear predominate. Some names, such as Manfield, Trueform and Freeman Hardy and Willis, are familiar to us today. So too are such well-known stores as Selfridges, Kendal Milne, Peter Robinson and the Co-op, which all had large boot departments. Other names, however, have long since disappeared. Shoe products for the care or repair of footwear were also advertised: 'Sandringham Boot Cream', 'Meltonian for Good Shoes', and 'The Wood-Milne Rubber Heel Pads'. Buttonhooks, in particular, carry advertisements for a variety of other items including, 'Nestles Milk', 'Robinsons Patent Groats for Invalids', 'Dr Lovelace's Soap', 'Holloway's Pills and Ointment' and 'Homepride Self-raising Flour'. Occasionally the handle bears the simple statement 'Your Change With Thanks', and was either given away with a purchase, or in place of a farthing change.

There are other variations where the buttonhook slides up, or is revealed when a cylindrical case is opened. Again buttonhook and shoehorn might be combined, in which case the buttonhook is usually a simple steel loop, with the shoehorn of metal or plastic carrying the message. Others advertise shops and companies in Europe, Canada and the USA, a reminder of the early twentieth century travelling boom.

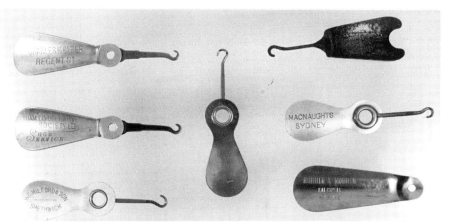

Combined advertising shoehorns and buttonhooks. Left: Three aluminium shoehorns with swivelling steel buttonhooks: 'Charles H Baber, Regent St'; 'B'ham Co-operative Society Ltd, Shoe Service'; 'H. C. Milford & Son, Smethwick'. Brass shoehorn, 'Wear "K" Shoes', with swivelling steel buttonhook. Right: 'Compliments of Hotel Vendome, San Jose California'; 'Macnaughts Sydney'; 'Robbin & Robbin, Kalispell, Montana'.

Assorted advertisement styles. Left: Three spat hooks with looped handles: ' "Standard" Spats'; 'Bond Street Spats'; 'Wear Carley's Boots estab 1832'. Top: Three examples advertising theatres: 'Leicester Palace Theatre'; 'Shepherds Bush Empire Theatre'; 'Hackney Empire Theatre'. Right: The buttonhook in these three examples slides back inside the case: 'Vic Gunn, Phone Brighton 980'; 'Novelty for Advertisers' (this wording would have been used on samples to attract other would-be advertisers): 'Owbridges Lung Tonic for Coughs and Colds'. Bottom: Three pairs of linked puzzle hooks: 'Read Pearson's Weekly'; 'The Humorist 2d'; ' "Tidy Betty" Stove and Grate Polish'. Centre: 'Wear Salter & Salter's Boots'. In this example the buttonhook screws away inside the case.

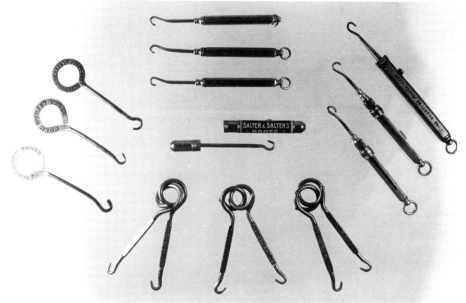

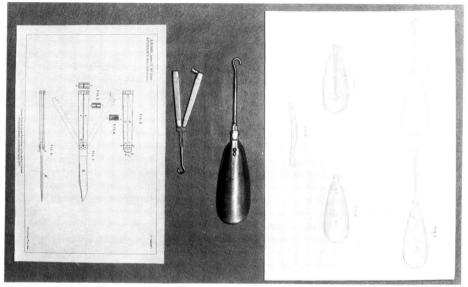

Kessler's patent of 1880 (left) showed an 'Improvement in springless clasp knives and other like articles'. Although the one illustrated contains a buttonhook, the examples most frequently found contain scissors. Sigmund Pulzer in 1882 filed his patent (right) for an 'Improved Combination Shoe-horn and Button-hook', with the buttonhook hinged at one end of the shoehorn, 'so that it may be folded up and conveniently carried in the pocket forming a most useful and compact companion'. This patent proved popular both in Britain and the USA.

In 1826, a patent was taken out by one Francis Halliday for an 'improved Bootjack'. The presence of a buttonhook, included in the specification, is mentioned only in passing, so it may be concluded that buttonhooks were objects well enough recognised in the 1820s for them to require no further explanation. From Victorian times, many buttonhook and shoehorn variations were patented both in Britain and the USA, though some were far-fetched and impractical, and probably never produced.

There are a number of patents concerning the dainty glovehooks carried by ladies, and others which combine buttonhooks with knives, pencil sharpeners, pens and pencils. Several travelling brushes were invented, which open to reveal useful items, including buttonhooks. Although unfastening was not a great problem, several patents were granted for appliances which combined an aid for both fastening and unfastening buttons.

The idea for a buttonhook combined with a puzzle was invented by Lester in 1888, who constructed 'a buttonhook of metal or wire... for use upon buttons of boots, leggings, gloves and for other similar purposes'. Those produced often carry advertisements. Examples include 'Tidy Betty Stove and Grate Polish', and 'Pearson's Weekly', a popular magazine of the 1890s. Awkward collar fastenings were not forgotten. In 1897, Taylor patented 'An Improved Stud or Buttonhook'. Later, in 1904, Bhisey invented another 'Improved Device for use in Fastening Collars, Gloves, Boots or the like'.

During the 1920s, shoehorn patents frequently included buttonhooks. In 1923, Richards patented the ingenious idea of combining both a buttonhook and a shoehorn with a pair of metal boot or shoe trees. The aim of most of these inventions was to improve on the basic buttonhook and shoehorn and provide an item that was compact and easily portable.

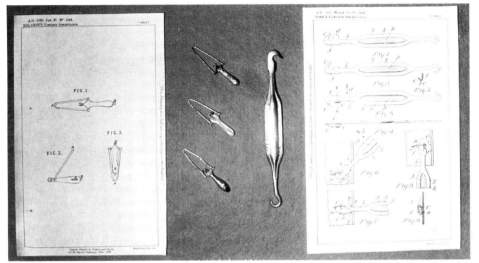

In 1888 Rolason patented his idea for a buttonhook with a hinged wire to close over the handle and spring into a small slot on either side of it when not required for use. This type of glovehook (left), was quite widely produced, usually in silver, and has other variations such as the mother-of-pearl handle (centre left), and fish-shaped handle (bottom left). In 1905, Arthur York, a boot manufacturer of Wolverhampton, invented a buttonhook with one end adapted to aid unbuttoning. He maintained that one of the chief objections to the wearing of leather leggings, and also boots and shoes that were fastened by means of buttons and buttonholes, was the difficulty experienced in unfastening them. His device included a shaped piece of metal, which, when pushed through the buttonhole, forced the button back through it. York's patent came into production under the trade mark ' "Sesame" the "Unbutton" Hook', but was not widely used as, on the whole, unbuttoning did not cause many problems.

BUTTONHOOKS AND SHOEHORNS TODAY

Demand for shoehorns today is mainly from shoeshops who, as with shoemakers centuries ago, still provide this aid when their customers try on footwear. Modern examples are usually of plastic, but ornamental shoehorns in brass and other materials are available in gift shops and the like, and many homes can still produce a shoehorn if required.

Abbey Horn, of Kendal in Cumbria — one of the few remaining horners in the world — still use traditional craftsmanship to make a wide range of horn items, including shoehorns, as they have done for over 200 years. Each year they make two long shoehorns which are presented to the Lord Mayor and Lady Mayoress of London by a livery company, the Worshipful Company of Horners. Such long shoehorns are a speciality of the makers and are among many

products which they export. Apart from requiring great skill to make, shoehorns up to 3 feet (0.9 m) long can prove most useful to those who are infirm or arthritic. For the more extravagant, the *Sunday Times* suggested at Christmas 1975, 'Treat them to a £677 gold shoehorn from Aspreys'.

As early as 1925, the *Lotus and Delta News* proclaimed 'GOOD-BYE BUTTONHOOK!" at the head of an article extolling the virtues of the new press-button fastening invented for their latest bar-shoes. But, despite their forecast, the buttonhook struggled on until the early 1940s, when its useful life, in decline for a decade, finally ended. Some forty years later it is regarded as a curio. The buttonhook, however, well used to fluctuating fortunes over the centuries, did not completely die. In simple utilitarian form it is still made today, and sold in varying quantities in Britain and other countries. Scottish Highland regiments, both in Britain and Canada are supplied with buttonhooks to fasten their gaiters. Startrite still place a buttonhook in every box of children's button-bar shoes sent to Europe, America and Canada.

The theatre too has played its part, for although some of the button-boots used in period productions have concealed zip-fasteners, others still use buttons and, of course, still require a buttonhook to fasten them. In 1978, the actor James Mason, being interviewed about his role as Dr Watson in a Sherlock Holmes film, was toying with a buttonhook. When questioned about it he replied 'I have someone to do up my boots, but I could do it myself. As a small boy in Huddersfield it used to give me great pleasure to fasten my father's boots'.

Strangely enough, the buttonhook today occasionally comes to the aid of the zip-fastener. Invented in 1924 as an alternative to buttons, hooks and laces, the zip helped to hasten the buttonhook's decline. Long back zips on dresses can be very hard to reach; a buttonhook caught in the loop makes it much easier to grasp, and speedily accomplishes the fastening. In some shoeshops, too, the assistants are provided with buttonhooks, saving wear and tear on their finger-nails when pulling up the long zips on customers' tight-fitting fashion boots.

This perhaps seems something of an ignoble end for the buttonhook, manufactured in such profusion and so essential such a relatively short time ago. But what of the future? Given the whimsical nature of the fashion world, it is always possible that the buttonhook could again come into its own. For, as observed in *The Noble Gentleman* of 1647:
'Nothing is thought rare
Which is not new, and followed: yet we

The late James Mason demonstrating the present day art of using a buttonhook. The photograph was taken in 1979 outside Elstree Studios where he was filming the Sherlock Holmes mystery 'Murder by Decree'. Mr Mason, in his role as Dr Watson, used a steel fold-over buttonhook to fasten his boots.

know
That what was worn some twenty years ago,
Comes into grace again'.

FURTHER READING

Betensley, Bertha. *Antique Buttonhooks for Shoes, Gloves and Clothing*. Educator Press, USA, 1975. Reprinted by the Buttonhook Society, 1991.

Betensley, Bertha. *Buttonhooks to Trade, to Treasure*. USA, 1958. Reprinted by the Buttonhook Society, 1992.

The Buttonhook Society. *The Boutonneur*. A bi-monthly illustrated newsletter sent to members: s.a.e. please to Honorary Secretary and Editor, Paul Moorhead, 83 Loose Road, Maidstone, Kent ME15 7DA.

Compton, Sylvia L. *Buttonhooks, Collecting and Price Guide*. Andrew Black and Associates, USA, 1983. Available in the United Kingdom from the Buttonhook Society.

Cumming, Valerie. *Gloves* (The Costume Accessories Series). B. T. Batsford, 1983.

Cunnington, C. W. and P. *Handbook of English Costume in the Nineteenth Century*. Faber and Faber, 1959.

Johnson, Eleanor. *Fashion Accessories*. Shire, 1980, reprinted 1994.

Swann, June. *Shoes* (The Costume Accessories Series). B. T. Batsford, 1982.

Wilson, Eunice. *A History of Shoe Fashions*. Pitman, 1970.

PLACES TO VISIT

Blaise Castle House Museum, Henbury, Bristol BS10 7QS. Telephone: 01179 506789.

Dundee Art Galleries and Museums, Albert Square, Dundee, Scotland DD1 1DA. Telephone: 01382 434000.

The Gallery of English Costume, Platt Hall, Rusholme, Manchester M14 5LL. Telephone: 0161-224 5217.

The Museum of London, London Wall, London EC2Y 5HN. Telephone: 0171-600 3699.

Northampton Museums and Art Gallery, Guildhall Road, Northampton NN1 1DP. Telephone: 01604 39415.

The Shoe Museum, C. and J. Clark Ltd, Street, Somerset BA16 0YA. Telephone: 01458 43131.

Worthing Museum and Art Gallery, Chapel Road, Worthing, West Sussex BN11 1HD. Telephone: 01903 239999; museum shop: 01903 204229.

ACKNOWLEDGEMENTS

The author gratefully acknowledges the help and encouragement given by her husband; the assistance in the research for this book from June Swann, shoe historian, and Paul Moorehead, Ron Mold and other members of The Buttonhook Society who, in contributing to their newsletter, have confirmed many of her original findings. She thanks the following museums and companies for help with photography and the loan of catalogues: Blaise Castle House Museum, C. and J. Clark Ltd, Dent-Fownes Ltd, C. G. Lambourne, I. and R. Morley, the Museum of London, Northampton Museum and Worthing Museum. Patents are reproduced by permission of The Comptroller, Patent Office, London. Special thanks are due to those who lent items for photography, and the antique dealers who, while encouraging her collecting, have become personal friends. Quotations from the following are acknowledged: Amy Stewart Fraser, *The Hills of Home*, Routledge and Kegan Paul, 1973; Alison Uttley, *The Button Box and Other Essays*, Faber and Faber; Therle Hughes, *Edwardiana for Collectors*, Therle Hughes, 1977, reproduced by permission of Curtis Brown Ltd.

Photographs are acknowledged as follows: Camera Five Four, Hale, Cheshire, pages 7 (top), 8 (top), 13 (both), 14, 15, 16, 21 (right); C. and J. Clark Ltd, page 21 (left); Stephen N. Harrington, Burchetts Green, Maidenhead, pages 2, 3, 5, 6, 7 (bottom), 8 (bottom), 9, 12 (both), 17, 18, 20 (both), 22 (bottom), 23, 24, 25, 27, 28 (top), 29, 30; Northampton Museum, pages 1, 10 (both); Worshipful Company of Horners/Museum of London, page 11. The photograph on page 8 (top) was originally published in *Antique Collectors' Club Magazine*.